Is My Hamster Wild?

The Secret Lives
of Hamsters, Gerbils
& Guinea Pigs

Rain Newcomb & Rose McLarney

LARK BOOKS

A Division of Sterling Publishing Co., Inc.
New York / London

Creative Director:
Celia Naranjo

Art Director:
Robin Gregory

Art Production Assistant:
Bradley Norris

Library of Congress Cataloging-in-Publication Data

Newcomb, Rain.
  Is my hamster wild? : the secret lives of hamsters, gerbils & guinea pigs
/ by Rain Newcomb & Rose McLarney. -- 1st ed.
     p. cm.
  Includes index.
  ISBN-13: 978-1-60059-242-3 (hc-plc with jacket : alk. paper)
  ISBN-10: 1-60059-242-2 (hc-plc with jacket : alk. paper)
  1. Hamsters as pets--Juvenile literature. 2. Gerbils as pets--Juvenile
literature. 3. Guinea pigs as pets--Juvenile literature. I. McLarney,
Rose, 1982- II. Title.
  SF459.H3N49 2008
  636.935--dc22

                           2007044312

10 9 8 7 6 5 4 3 2 1

First Edition

Published by Lark Books, A Division of Sterling Publishing Co., Inc., 387 Park Avenue South, New York, NY 10016

Text © 2008, Lark Books

Distributed in Canada by Sterling Publishing, c/o Canadian Manda Group, 165 Dufferin Street, Toronto, Ontario, Canada M6K 3H6

Distributed in the United Kingdom by GMC Distribution Services, Castle Place, 166 High Street, Lewes, East Sussex, England BN7 1XU

Distributed in Australia by Capricorn Link (Australia) Pty Ltd., P.O. Box 704, Windsor, NSW 2756 Australia

The written instructions, photographs, designs, patterns, and projects in this volume are intended for the personal use of the reader and may be reproduced for that purpose only. Any other use, especially commercial use, is forbidden under law without written permission of the copyright holder.

Every effort has been made to ensure that all the information in this book is accurate. However, due to differing conditions, tools, and individual skills, the publisher cannot be responsible for any injuries, losses, and other damages that may result from the use of the information in this book.

If you have questions or comments about this book, please contact: Lark Books, 67 Broadway, Asheville, NC 28801, 828-253-0467

Manufactured in China

ISBN 13: 978-1-60059-242-3
ISBN 10: 1-60059-242-2

For information about custom editions, special sales, premium and corporate purchases, please contact Sterling Special Sales Department at 800-805-5489 or specialsales@sterlingpub.com.

Contents

Cute Pet or Wild Animal?.....6

Gnawing Away.................. 8

Night & Day .... .10

All About Hamsters 12

A New Pet 14

Bears, Pandas & Dwarfs .... .16

A Real Mouthful............... .18

What's That Smell? 20

Home Sweet Home 22

Run (& Dig) for Cover 24

Hairless Little Hamsters 26

Wild is Wild................. 28

All About Gerbils........ 30

Gerbils: Great, Small & Fat (Tailed). . 32

It's a Gerbil's Life............. .34

On the Lookout & on the Run 36

Get Underground............... 38

Baby Gerbils .... .40

Who's Talking? 42

All About Guinea Pigs....... 44

More Kinds of Guinea Pigs! ...... .46

Those Crazy Relatives............48

Grazing on Grass................50

Family Life 52

Run, Swim, Hop—Fall Down ..... .54

What's My Guinea Pig Saying?.....56

A Historic Pet .... .58

Other Wild Relatives....... 60

Where Do Rodents Live? 62

Index.................. 64

I'm a hamster.

I'm a gerbil.

And I'm a guinea pig.

Cute Pet or Wild Animal?

There's a wild animal hiding inside your fuzzy friend! The hamsters, gerbils, and guinea pigs that live safe and snug in your house have relatives in the wild. They find food, build homes, play, and fight with each other outside in the natural world. And these wild animals have a lot in common with your pet.

Hamsters stuff their cheeks with food, but they aren't just being cute. They do it because no one feeds them in the wild. They have to find and store their own food. Gerbils don't burrow just for fun—they have to make their own shelter in the deserts. And guinea pigs aren't just making noise because they want to talk. In the wild, this is how they alert other guinea pigs to danger.

Although hamsters, gerbils, and guinea pigs are all rodents, they are very different from each other in many ways. Gerbils are the smallest—about 4 inches (10.2 cm) long—and hamsters are slightly larger—on average, about 6 inches (15.3 cm) long. Most gerbils have long tails with fur on them. Hamsters' tails are usually short and bare. Guinea pigs are much bigger than either hamsters or gerbils. They have thicker, stockier bodies and can be more than a foot (30.5 cm) long.

Understanding how your pet's wild relatives behave will unlock the mysteries of why your pet does what he does.

Gnawing Away

Does your pet gnaw on the bars of her cage or chew up her toys? She's not secretly trying to escape, and she doesn't hate her toys. Hamsters, gerbils, and guinea pigs, like all rodents, have teeth that never stop growing. Chewing on hard things wears down their teeth. If they don't have wood blocks or cardboard tubes to use for their teeth, they take matters into their own hands—or mouths.

Treat or toothbrush?

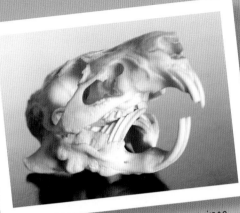

Look how big the teeth are on this guinea pig skull!

Prairie dogs eat plants in the spring and gnaw on seeds in the summer.

This squirrel likes seedy restaurants.

Beavers' teeth do more than cut food—they cut wood for building, too.

In the wild, rodents depend on their teeth. They eat tough foods like seeds and nuts. Some rodents, like beavers, use their teeth to cut down trees. Having teeth that constantly grow is a good thing, because the rodent will always have a mouthful of teeth when she needs them.

But there is a downside. If a rodent's teeth get too long, her mouth can't open and close correctly. Extremely overgrown teeth can cause a rodent to starve to death. So, rodents have to keep gnawing away.

Should I bite the hand that holds me?

NIGHT & Day

Do you wake up at night to the sounds of scurrying feet and nibbling teeth? Do you come home from school to a snoozing friend? Or is your pet wide awake and wanting to play when you are?

Hamsters, gerbils, and guinea pigs are active at different times of the day. Guinea pigs are diurnal, like you. That means they find food

I don't need a night-light—
I can see in the dark.

This guinea pig is up to see the sunrise (and maybe smell the flowers, too).

and play during the day. But hamsters and gerbils are nocturnal. They're most active at night, scampering and searching for food after the sun goes down. Their eyes can see in the dark and their whiskers help them feel around. Their senses of hearing and smell also work well at night. After a long night of scampering around, hamsters and gerbils sleep all day.

Hamsters and gerbils are nocturnal because they like to look for food when most of their predators are sleeping. Guinea pigs look for food when predators are awake, but they have their own ways of staying safe.

11

All About Hamsters

Are you talking about me?

Does your furry little friend have a secret life you don't know about? What's he thinking when he scurries around in his cage? Why does he bury himself in his bedding? Where is he trying to go when he runs on his wheel?

Not all hamsters live in cages in people's homes. There are lots of hamsters that live on their own, searching for food, making homes, and raising families. These wild hamsters live in Europe and Asia.

Whether they're living in the wild or in your living room, wild and pet hamsters have a lot in common. By learning more about what wild hamsters do to survive, you can learn more about what your hamster is doing right now.

We're on our best behavior for this picture.

Scoop a hamster up in your palm so that you won't hurt her—and she can't jump out.

A New Pet

Do you have a Syrian hamster? You probably do—most pet hamsters are Syrians. And here's the crazy thing: all Syrian hamsters come from the same family!

In 1930, a scientist found a nest of Syrian hamsters in—guess where?—Syria. He didn't know what they were, so he took the mother and babies to his lab to find out more about them. The hamsters bred there, and their offspring became the hamsters we have today. Few wild Syrian hamsters have been found since then. Scientists think they may be extinct. (There are plenty of other kinds of hamsters that still live in the wild though.)

I'm not going to ham it up for this photo.

What, you don't think I look like a wild beast?

About 15 years after the scientist found the first nest of hamsters, their descendants became popular pets.

Bears, Pandas
& Dwarfs

What kinds of hamsters have you seen? Syrian hamsters come in several different colors. Golden-colored Syrian hamsters are also called "honey bears." Black ones are called "black bears," white ones "polar bears," and black and white ones "panda bears." (But, since they're your pets, you can call them any name you want.)

Golden hamsters have light-colored fur on their stomachs.

Do I look like a panda bear to you?

16

Don't call me gray—I prefer dove-colored.

If it were snowing, I'd blend right in.

There are 17 more types of hamsters, and each one has different colors of fur, too. Most have brown, almost red, or gray fur with white, gray, or black stomachs. These colors help hamsters blend in with their natural environment, making it harder for predators to see them.

During the winter, the Winter White hamster's gray fur turns white. That's because the hamster is getting ready to hide in the snow.

Does your hamster have a stripe down his back? In the wild, this is excellent camouflage. The stripe disguises the shape of the hamster, so that he's not so obvious to predators.

A Real Mouthful

Hamsters stuff all the food they can find in pouches inside their cheeks. They keep cramming food into their mouths until their cheeks stick out way past their shoulders! But your hamster's not a pig—she's hoarding her food to store it, just like wild hamsters do.

In the wild, hamsters use their cheeks to carry food back to their burrows where they store it for later. Hamsters know that when winter comes, they won't be able to find food. They keep food in their houses so they'll always have plenty to eat. Have you ever found piles of food tucked in the nesting material when you cleaned out your hamster's cage? She's saving it for later, because her wild instincts are telling her that someday the food might run out.

Hamsters don't get in trouble for eating with their hands.

18

Gimme that human food!

This hamster looks like she's about to pop!

How am I going to carry all of this?

Squirrels, porcupines, and many other rodents store food for the winter. But most of them have to put food in storage one piece at a time. Lucky rodents, such as hamsters and chipmunks, have cheek pouches that let them carry more. In fact, a Syrian hamster can carry more than her own body weight worth of food in her cheek pouches!

Chipmunk cheeks!

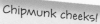

What's That
Smell?

Do we have to talk about MY personal hygiene?

If you were a hamster, you'd never have to bathe again...in water! Instead, you'd take a nice, scratchy sand bath when you were dirty. Most hamsters live in the desert, so they have to clean themselves using sand.

Even after a sand bath, your hamster will still stink a bit, and he'll look a little greasy. He's supposed to smell! In the wild, hamsters tell each other apart by their unique smells. They let other hamsters know where they live by releasing smelly oils from their scent glands. (If you clean your hamster's cage too well, he might not remember that this is his home, so leave a little bit of his old nesting materials in place.)

Home is where the stink is.

Hamsters aren't the only rodents that take sand baths. Their cousins, the chinchillas, roll in sand to clean their coats, too. In fact, getting wet can make these rodents sick. Give your furry friends bowls of special sand to roll in.

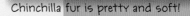
Chinchilla fur is pretty and soft!

Home Sweet Home

Does your hamster dig around in her cage, tunneling through her bedding? She's not trying to hide from you—she's obeying her wild instincts!

Wild hamsters make their homes in the dry, open land of Europe and Asia. It's hard to live there. It gets very cold, sometimes there's no food, and there are always predators that want to eat hamsters and their babies.

Do you like what I've done with the place? It was just a hole in the ground when I moved in.

There are many rooms in a hamster burrow. They have living rooms, bathrooms, and rooms for sleeping, just like your house. Hamsters also have special rooms for storing food. The food they store will help them survive droughts and harsh winters when the plants they eat don't grow. These rooms are connected by tunnels. Does your hamster have tubes in her cage? These will feel like tunnels to her.

Now, you're really butting in!

So, hamsters stay safe and warm by making their homes underground. They either dig burrows, or they move into an abandoned burrow and make it their own. When a pet hamster tunnels through her bedding, she's trying to make a burrow.

Sometimes I get lost on the way to the bathroom.

23

I'm really sticking my neck out here.

Run
(& Dig)
for Cover

Does your hamster race in his wheel all night long? In the wild, hamsters literally run for their lives. A fast scurry will keep them safe from the snakes and birds of prey that would like to snack on a tasty little hamster.

Wild hamsters also run around looking for food for hours each night. Your hamster is safe and well-fed in his cage, so he has to do something with his natural urge to run. Playing is his favorite way to use up all that extra energy.

Dive for cover!

Peekaboo.

Hamsters have another secret weapon to keep them safe—their claws. But they don't use their claws to fight off predators. (Hamsters are too little for that.) Instead, they dig burrows so they can hide below ground. Their short legs make it easier for them to scramble through the tight tunnels in their homes.

Many other rodents, like this marmot, dig burrows to keep themselves and their families safe.

Hairless

Little Hamsters

Animal babies don't mind being carried this way.

Have you ever seen a mother hamster stuffing babies into her cheeks? She's probably not eating them—she's hiding or carrying them to another location because she feels they are in danger.

Baby hamsters are born blind and hairless. They can have more than 12 siblings. Their mother puts them in the nest she built and nurses them for about a week. In about a month, they will be grown-up and will leave to live alone.

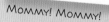

MOMMY! MOMMY!

Sometimes hamster mothers do eat their babies, but they don't do it because they're mean. These mothers are actually protecting their families. A sick baby will make the whole family sick, and if there are too many babies, there won't be enough food or space for everyone.

This piece of broccoli is bigger than me. Oh, lucky day!

Wild is

Wild

Are you my dinner?

Some hamsters eat insects, rodents, lizards, and even small birds!

Although they look cute and cuddly, hamsters can be ferocious. Being fierce keeps wild hamsters and their families alive.

In nature, hamsters have to defend their homes and food from other hamsters that try to move in. Hamsters will attack each other and sometimes fight to the death. Your pet will do this if you put a strange hamster in his cage.

Dwarf hamsters are the exception. They like to live together, and are very social.

Has your hamster ever bitten you when you picked him up? Don't be mad. He thought you were a predator, scooping him up to eat him. Give your hamster plenty of time to recognize your smell and learn to trust you.

Take that!

There's a paw-fight breaking out.

Tired or mad? Don't get close enough to find out.

Different gerbils have different tail lengths, fur colors, and markings.

All About

Gerbils

You wake up in the middle of the night. A loud THUMP THUMP THUMP sound is coming from your gerbil's cage. Then you hear her scurrying around her cage. You look over and she's standing on her hind legs, sniffing the air. What's going on?

Your gerbil is just doing the same things she'd be doing in the wild in Africa, India, and Asia—but she's doing it in her cage in your room. Wild gerbils don't have helpful humans around to bring them yummy food, keep them safe from predators, and give them cozy beds. They have to do that all by themselves.

Sand, rocks, and thorny plants make me feel right at home.

Most of the time, gerbils like to be together.

Your gerbil has a lot in common with the gerbils living in the wild. Knowing what wild gerbils do to survive will help you understand why your gerbil does the things she does.

I'm a tiny Dipodil gerbil.

Gerbils: Great, Small & **Fat** (Tailed)

What color is your gerbil? Gerbil fur can be all sorts of colors—black, white, brown, and shades that breeders call fox, nutmeg, dove, and lilac. But don't be fooled by the fancy names. The color of a gerbil's fur isn't for fashion—it's to keep him safe from predators!

When a gerbil's fur is the same color as his environment, it makes it harder for hungry predators to see him. Some gerbils have spots or special markings called points on their faces and feet like Siamese cats. These markings help gerbils blend in with their surroundings.

Gerbils are also known as sand rats, but I prefer to be called sandy blond.

32

Gerbils can stand up on their back feet, but they're still pretty short.

There are more than 100 kinds of gerbils and they're all different colors and sizes. In the wild, the Great gerbil is over a foot (30.2 cm) long. The charming Dipodil is just a quarter of that size.

Calling a gerbil "fat-tailed" isn't an insult—it's actually the name of a special kind of gerbil. Fat-tailed gerbils store digested food and water in their tails to help them survive in the Sahara Desert where they live. With all that inside, no wonder their tails look fat!

I'm named Great gerbil because I'm so big.

It's a Gerbil's *Life*

Maybe my buddies won't notice this carrot and I won't have to share.

Does your gerbil dig holes and hide food in her woodchips? She's acting like a wild gerbil that digs a burrow and stores food for her family.

Like hamsters, wild gerbils stay safe and warm in their underground homes. If you could peek inside a wild gerbil burrow, you might see gerbils bathing each other, playfully wrestling and chasing, and sleeping on top of each other in piles.

When it's cold and snowy, gerbils don't have to leave their cozy burrows. They can eat in for more than a week, using stored food. That's because after gerbils fill up on plants, seeds, nuts, roots, or insects, they put the leftovers away in their burrows for later. Pet gerbils hide food in their woodchips—they don't know that winter doesn't come to cages.

Wild gerbils share their burrows. Sometimes, when they feel crowded, they scratch and bite each other. But mostly, gerbils like to be around other gerbils. That's why, unlike a hamster, a pet gerbil that lives by herself might get lonely.

Hold the blind mice jokes—we're gerbils and we can see.

Hawks, eagles, owls, snakes, lizards, and weasels love to eat gerbils for breakfast, lunch, and dinner. Luckily, the little gerbil is far from helpless!

Gerbils are great runners. Their strong back legs help them run fast and jump far. Their feet also help them out. A gerbil's front feet have four toes each, but his back feet have five. It's not an accident—it's an advantage. Using those extra toes for support, he can stand on his back two feet like a prairie dog to look for danger. His long, furry tail helps him keep his balance.

It's time to take a stand—
I need more raisins.

Prairie dogs stand up to look around, just like gerbils.

Nothing can make a meal out of your gerbil when he's safe and cozy in his cage. But what is he going to do with all that energy he would have used to outrun enemies and search for food in the wild? Your gerbil will run around his cage, sniff the air anyway, and, if he's really lucky, take his plastic exercise ball out for a spin!

These leaves will make
a soft nest for me.

Get Underground

Does your pet gerbil dig in her cozy nesting materials? She's just following her instincts to make a burrow.

It's tough to be a wild gerbil. They live in the deserts, mountains, and plains, and they always have to look out for predators. To protect themselves from their enemies and to stay safe and warm, gerbils dig burrows, like hamsters.

If you have pet gerbils, you can give them cardboard and paper bags to shred and make into nests.

Sometimes gerbils make tunnels to connect their burrows. Sometimes there's just a single burrow. But whether a gerbil calls a burrow or a cage her home, she will always make herself a soft, cozy bed.

Wild gerbils can excavate so much that they make the ground cave in or kill plants growing above.

Baby Gerbils

Make sure your gerbils' cages are big enough. Otherwise, your gerbils might feel crowded and attack each other.

Whether they're wild or pets, all baby gerbils are helpless. They're born hairless and blind. They start moving around within a few days of birth—before their eyes open. When baby gerbils run and jump, it's cute. But they can also scamper right into (and off of) things and hurt themselves. Being inside the burrow protects the babies.

Mom? Is that you?

Baby squirrels stay safe in their nests high up in trees.

A litter of as many as 10 gerbil babies live with their mother and father. Parent gerbils sometimes eat their babies, but like hamsters, they're just doing what they have to to keep the rest of the family healthy. Gerbils are good parents that feed, cuddle, and play with their babies.

It's hard to tell gerbils and mice apart when they're born.

Who's Talking?

Hear THUMP THUMP THUMP coming from your gerbil's cage? Someone's trying to talk to you!

Gerbils have their own special way of communicating. They pound their long back feet on the ground, making a loud sound. The gerbil's family can hear and feel these thumps from far away.

What's your gerbil trying to say? Well, he might be warning his family that there's someone dangerous lurking around. Or, he could be telling them something exciting has happened—like really good food appearing in the food dish. He might just be saying hello and letting everybody know he's there. Sometimes young gerbils like to make noise just because they can.

I own this table. I rubbed my tummy all over it!

Does your gerbil drag his stomach over things? He's making an announcement that those things are his. Gerbils have special scent glands on their stomachs. When one gerbil rubs his stomach on something, other gerbils know that it belongs to him because of the way it smells!

Prairie dogs bark when there's danger.

Beavers have their own way of talking—they slap their tails on the water when they sense danger.

43

All About
Guinea Pigs

Even among the same breed, guinea pigs can have many different colors of coats.

Can you believe all of these different-looking creatures are guinea pigs? Guinea pigs have been pets for a long time. During that time, people have bred them to have many kinds of hair.

I have natural style.

You can have a guinea pig with long hair, short hair, curly hair, kinky hair, silky hair, hair that sticks out in all directions, or hair that grows so long it tangles. But no matter what your guinea pig looks like, she still has a lot in common with the wild guinea pigs that live in Central and South America.

I'm a two-toned guinea pig.

Guinea pigs enjoy each other's company, talk to each other, and eat their own poop because all of these things keep them safe and healthy in the wild. Knowing what guinea pigs do in the wild will help you understand what your guinea pig does at home.

Groom me!

No matter what its coat looks like, you can recognize a guinea pig by its stocky body and short tail and neck.

More Kinds of Guinea Pigs!

My hair is supposed to be messy.

Smooth-coated Agouti guinea pigs look like wild guinea pigs.

There are four types of wild guinea pigs. They are: the Brazilian guinea pig, the Shiny guinea pig, the Montane guinea pig, and the Greater guinea pig. Guinea pigs that live in the wild don't have crazy long hair. (It would get in the way.) Their fur helps camouflage them so they can hide from predators.

Guinea pigs can be all one color, two colors, or up to three different colors. Their fur can be all different textures and lengths, too.

There are lots of breeds of guinea pigs that people keep as pets. The Peruvian's hair can get to be more than a foot (30.2 cm) long, growing toward and falling over her face.

Some pet owners keep their Peruvian guinea pigs' hair in curlers so it doesn't knot!

The White Crested guinea pig has a white spot on the top of its head. The Texel guinea pig has curly hair. The Abyssinian's fur has cowlicks and sticks out in all directions. The Teddy's fur is kinky and fuzzy.

This is a Coronet guinea pig.

Guess what the Silkie guinea pig's fur feels like.

My fur won't get tangled in this grass.

Peruvian guinea pigs always live in a hairy situation.

Those Crazy Relatives

Coypus are also called nutrias.

In many parts of the world, guinea pigs are called cavies. That's because they're part of the Caviidae family. Guinea pigs have lots of unusual relatives.

The largest rodent in the world is one of them. The capybara weighs more than 100 pounds (45.4 kg). (Next to a capybara, the 3-pound [1.4 kg] guinea pig would look tiny!) The capybara spends a lot of his time in the water. His feet are webbed to make him a better swimmer.

Another relative of the guinea pig, the coypu, also likes the water, but he's much smaller than the capybara. He doesn't get any larger than 20 pounds (9 kg), but he sticks out in other ways—his long, bright orange teeth stick out of his mouth! And females have nipples on their backs so that babies can nurse when their mother is swimming.

The agouti is a 13-pound (5.9 kg) cavy that, like the guinea pig, doesn't live in the water. Instead, his special feet are built for galloping around the forest and burying nuts. He has only three toes on each back foot and big claws like horse hooves.

Capybaras eat 6 to 8 pounds (2.7 to 3.6 kg) of grass every day.

Agoutis can live for as long as 20 years.

GRAZING on Grass

Have you seen your guinea pig eat her poop? It might gross you out, but it's actually very healthy for her. In fact, guinea pigs can get sick if they don't eat their poop. In order to get all the vitamins out of the plants she eats, a guinea pig has to digest her food twice, and the only way to do that is by eating her poop.

Wild guinea pigs walk around nibbling on plants all day. They're very good at remembering long, complicated paths to the tastiest food.

Guinea pigs have to go out in the open to find food, where it's easy for predators to see them. So, they graze in groups called herds. Eating with a lot of other guinea pigs helps keep them safer. There are more eyes and ears on the lookout for danger. And when a predator attacks, the whole herd scatters, which makes it harder for the predator to catch somebody.

Every meal is a salad bar for guinea pigs—they live on plants.

Wild guinea pigs live in places where there are plants to eat all year long, so they don't have to store food like hamsters and gerbils. They get all the water they need from the plants they eat, so they don't have to go out looking for a drink either. But pet guinea pigs need water because they eat dry food.

It's not just cows and horses that eat hay. Pet guinea pigs do, too.

Hmmm...should I eat the blade of grass on the right first? Or the blade on the left?

Family
Life
· · · · · · ·

Three's a crowd—and more is even better.

Does your guinea pig get sad when you're gone? Is he excited when you come home from school? Guinea pigs are social animals that love their families, so your guinea pig is very attached to you. His excellent sense of smell and good hearing help him recognize you.

Wild guinea pigs live in herds, so they have to get along. One male is usually in charge of a herd. If any of the other guinea pigs try to challenge him or compete for attention from the females, the leader and the other guinea pig will fight. But mostly, guinea pigs like each other's company and get along.

The whole herd helps keep the babies safe from predators. There are lots of eyes and noses to keep a lookout for danger. Mothers can have as many as 13 babies at a time, though they usually have fewer. Guinea pig babies are born out in the open, not in the safety of a burrow like hamster and gerbil babies. They have to be able to move with the herd right away. The babies have fur, and can see and run a few hours after birth. They're also much bigger than hamster and gerbil babies. In fact, a newborn guinea pig is about the same size as a full-grown hamster.

Best friends.

I may be bigger than a hamster, but I'm still a baby.

53

Run, Swim, Hop— Fall Down

This flower smelled better than it tastes.

Unlike many other rodents, guinea pigs seem kind of clumsy. Though gerbils, hamsters, squirrels, rats, porcupines, and other rodents are great at climbing and leaping, guinea pigs fall off things a lot.

Guinea pigs seem clumsy because their eyes are on the sides of their heads. They can't see straight ahead and don't judge height and distance very well. But their eyes are this way for a good reason—they can see in almost every direction at once. This helps them notice predators that are trying to sneak up on them.

When guinea pigs spot a predator, they run for safety. This is something they're very good at—they're fast and tricky, too. They twist, turn, and wedge themselves in crevices and under things to keep from becoming somebody's next meal.

Take a left at the second flower, cross the root, and you'll find the YUMMIEST patch of weeds.

Guinea pigs can also swim. They don't enjoy swimming like their relatives the capybaras, and it's not healthy for them to be wet. But they can swim to safety if they fall in water.

Capybaras are better at swimming than guinea pigs. They can even dive.

And guinea pigs have a special move no other rodents have—popcorning. Have you seen your guinea pig hop up and down, skip, and throw her legs in the air? That's popcorning. It's not a way of trying to escape from anything— your guinea pig is just happy to be alive!

They're both rodents, but a guinea pig could never climb a tree like this porcupine.

What's My Guinea Pig Saying?

Because guinea pigs hang out together, they talk to each other—a lot. They have something to say about almost every situation. They rumble, chirp, grunt, squeal, coo, hiss, and more. They tell each other when there's danger, and when there's good food nearby.

When they're excited, they make the sound "wheet!" A guinea pig might wheet to get the attention of other guinea pigs, to point out something interesting, or because she needs help. Pet guinea pigs wheet when they see their owner.

I'm purr-fectly happy.

What did you just say?

Grunting and gnashing teeth means your guinea pig is being ferocious and wants to scare something (or someone) away.

Guinea pigs coo to reassure one another that all is well. Older guinea pigs usually coo to babies.

Does your guinea pig purr when you hold her? That means she's happy. She may also purr when she's bathing or eating something really yummy.

That's right—I'm talking to you!

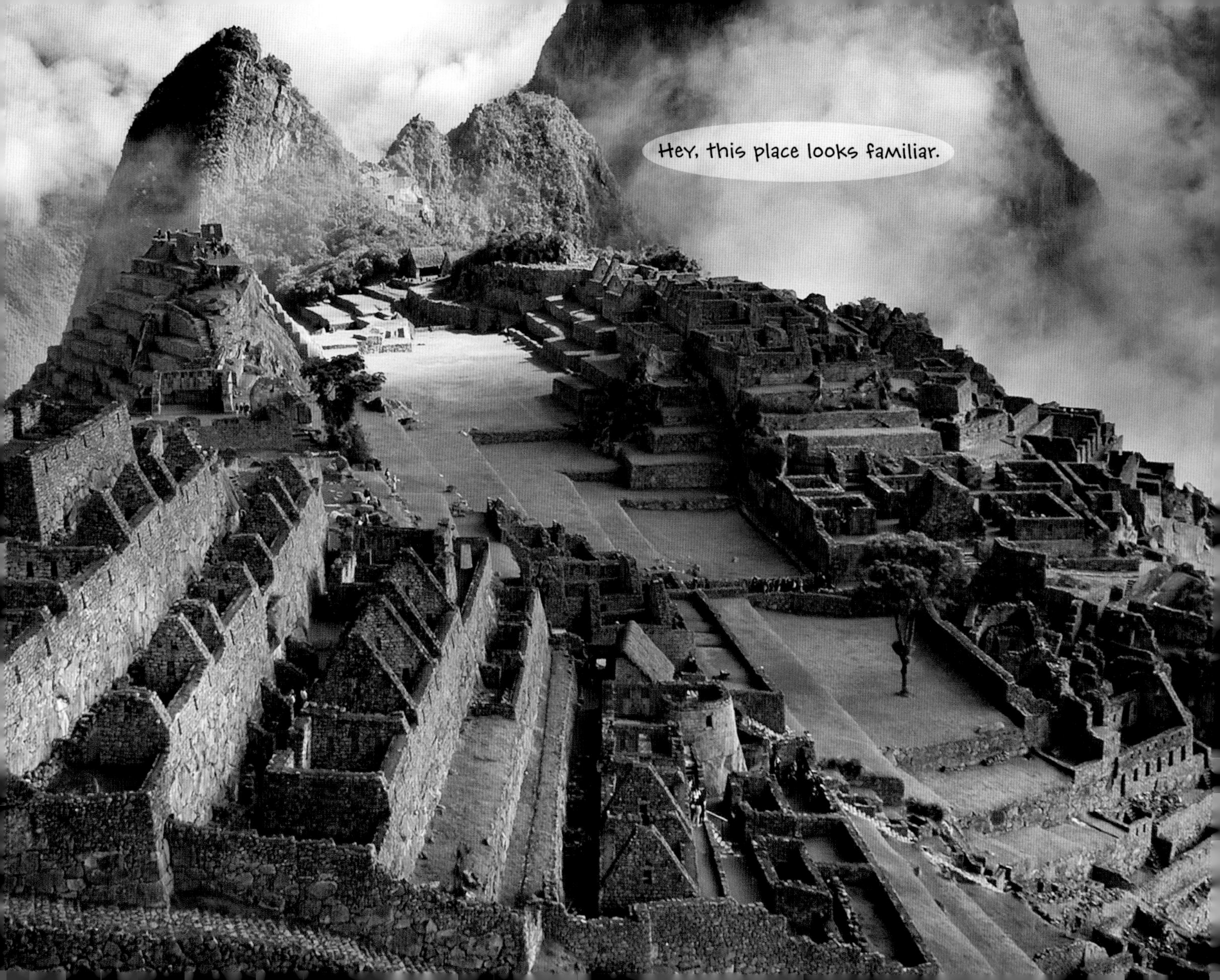
Hey, this place looks familiar.

A HISTORIC Pet

My family is from Machu Picchu—we've been civilized for thousands of years longer than you.

If you have a guinea pig, you're in good company. Queen Elizabeth I had a pet guinea pig, and so did President Teddy Roosevelt. Guinea pigs became popular pets in Europe in the 1500s.

In Peru, people have been taking care of guinea pigs for more than 3,000 years. The guinea pigs that lived in the famous, ancient city of Machu Picchu weren't too different from the guinea pig in your living room. But Peruvian guinea pigs weren't just pets—Incas raised them for meat. Guinea pigs taste like chicken or rabbit.

In Peru, Bolivia, and Ecuador, people still eat guinea pigs. Peruvians eat about 65 million guinea pigs every year. The animals may roam around in the countryside or live urban lives. In Peruvian cities, owners build houses for guinea pigs on the roofs of buildings.

Other

Wild Relatives

You may not recognize me in my natural environment, but I'm still a rat.

You're probably familiar with a few of your pet's other close relatives, such as rats, mice, and squirrels. But did you know that there are more than 2,000 different kinds of rodents in the world?

Rodents evolved right after the dinosaurs became extinct. And the first rodents were huge! One of the guinea pig's ancestors weighed 1,545 pounds (700.1 kg) and was as large as a buffalo. And there were giant 8-foot (2.4 m) long beavers wandering around North America.

Today's rodents are much smaller than their ancestors, although some might still seem big to you. Rodents can look very different from one another.

Eeek! A mouse!!!
Oh wait, that's me.

Here are just a few of your pet's wild relatives.

Have you seen my acorn? I know I left it right here.

Many jerboas are only 5 inches (12.7 cm) long.

Everybody wants to touch the super-soft chinchilla.

Poor porcupine—nobody ever wants to pet him.

The capybara can be more than 4 feet (1.2 m) long.

Where Do Rodents Live?

Squirrels make their homes in trees and spend most of their time off the ground.

Rodents live everywhere in the world, except one place: Antarctica. And that entire continent is covered in ice, so who's counting?

Rodents make their homes next to ponds and streams, in deserts, in the woods, in the city, on farmland, in mountains, on grassy plains, and everywhere in between. If you have a pet hamster, gerbil, or guinea pig, you know the best rodent in the world is the one that lives in your home.

Now that you know hamsters, gerbils, guinea pigs, and their wild relatives are similar, you can find out even more about your pet's secret life. Watch her every day and compare what she does to how rodents behave in nature. Have fun discovering your pet's wild side!

Prairie dogs like to live on the wide-open grassland.

Muskrats live next to the water.

Kangaroo rats make their homes in the desert.

Beavers build their homes next to water, too.

Pacas live in tropical forests.

Some marmots live in the mountains.

Index

Abyssinian guinea pig, 47
Agouti guinea pig, 46, 49
Alpaca, 46
Babies, 26-27, 40-41, 52-53
Bathing, hamster, 20-21
Beaver, 9, 63
Black bear hamsters, 16
Brazilian guinea pig, 46
Burrow, 22-23, 24-25, 34-35, 38-39

Capybara, 49, 55, 61
Cheek pouches, hamster, 18-19
Chinchilla, 21, 61
Chipmunk, 19
Coronet guinea pig, 47
Coypu, 48-49

Dipodil, 33
Diurnal, 10-11,
Domestication, 14-15, 59

Fat-tailed gerbil, 33
Fighting, 29, 35, 53
Food, 18-19, 34-35, 50-51
Fur, 16-17, 32-33, 45-47

Gerbil, 30-43, varieties of, 32-33
Golden hamster, 16
Great gerbil, 33
Greater guinea pig, 46
Guinea pig, 44-59, varieties of, 45-47

Hamster, 12-29, varieties of, 16-17
Herd, 50, 53
Honey bear hamster, 16

Introduction, 6-7

Jerboa, 61

Kangaroo rat, 63

Marmot, 63
Mice, 41, 60
Montane guinea pig, 46
Muskrat, 63

Native habitat, 13, 22, 31, 45, 58-59, 62-63
Nocturnal, 10-11

Paca, 63
Panda bear hamster, 16
Peruvian guinea pig, 46, 47
Polar bear hamster, 16
Porcupine, 19, 55, 61
Prairie dog, 9, 37, 63

Rodents, 60-63
Running, 36-37, 54

Scent, 21, 43
Shiny guinea pig, 46
Silkie guinea pig, 45
Size, 7
Sounds, 42-43, 56-57
Squirrel, 9, 18, 41, 61, 62
Swimming, 55
Syrian hamster, 14-15, 16

Tails, 7, 33, 37, 43
Teddy guinea pig, 47
Teeth, 8-9
Texel guinea pig, 47
Thumping, 30, 42

White crested guinea pig, 47
Winter White hamster, 17

Photo credits